DAVID JA

Any Cornish Beach

with very best wishes

David James

Bosorne Publications
St Just

First published in the United Kingdom in 2012 by
Bosorne Publications
The Count House, Bosorne, St Just, Cornwall
TR19 7NR

ISBN 978-0-9550087-1-9

Acknowledgements

My thanks to Les Merton, editor of *Poetry Cornwall* who first published *Any Cornish Beach*, *Let's Go Sailing* and *The Land's End*.

I am indebted to many people for their support and encouragement over the years.

Lucilla Napier gave me *Selected Poems* by DH Lawrence many years ago, *'to inspire but not to influence.'* Maggie O'Brien gave me the confidence to write. That is her wonderful painting on the front cover. Professor Peter Mudford encouraged me to publish these poems. Paula Newbery has been a most supportive poetry 'buddy'. George Szirtes, gifted poet and gentle tutor, helped me more than he will ever know on a memorable Arvon course. *Poets in Exile* is dedicated to George. My family insisted these poems were published.

I am especially grateful to Alice Kavounas, whose Poetry School Seminars did so much to help me and who is the editor of this volume.

Cover image *Any Cornish Beach* © Maggie O'Brien
The painting is in the author's collection

Printed by R. Booth Ltd.
The Praze, Penryn, Cornwall
TR10 8AA

CONTENTS

For Philippa, Jake and Ellie

ANY CORNISH BEACH

Let's go walking,
you and I,
to any Cornish beach
gleaming wetly,
race barefoot
on unmarked sand,
jump pools,
throw stones,
build a castle
where we stand,
not caring if the tide comes in.

WORDS

In the beginning was the word
echoing through empty wastes.
Listen!
It is still there, hanging in the air.
Or is that a bird?

Whispered to the night sky,
your words will soar among the pipistrelles
to join that first word,
and all the millions of mouthless words
spoken since time began,
an unheard babel,
the earth song of birth,
death's sobbing lament,
all life in between.
So many words.

At the end,
all that remains is the word.

MARCH STORM

It is the last big tide.
In a pale washed sky
a sickle moon holds
the dying storm
in the hollow of her hand

REMEMBERING A SUMMER STORM

Out of a clear blue sky
a sudden, vicious squall
knocked us flat,
swamped the crew.
We struggled with sails,
pumped for our lives,
saved the ship
and each other.

It blew day after day,
battered people and gear.
We'd nowhere to run
so we sailed close-hauled,
watch and watch about.
Watch and watch about
we cared for the ship
and for each other.

As the storm eased
to a gale, then a breeze,
we hove to, took stock,
slept, watch and watch about,
then shook out the reefs,
sailed on, running free,
caring for the ship
and for each other.

LET'S GO SAILING

Let's go sailing
you and I
slipping out one ebbing tide
with a fair wind –
even if it rains
it won't matter
because we won't look back –

we'll blow like feathers
in our walnut shell
cresting the deep Atlantic swell
and watch ships –
but mostly each other

we'll sail through rainbows
breaking around the bows
and kiss salt from lips and eyes
and wonder, sometimes,
how deep the water is.

ANCHORING

I.

Mahé, Seychelles 1969

Link after hand-forged link
roared through the hawse pipe,
rust clouds smoking over the fo'c'stle,
lay stretched out
in ten clear fathoms
on a fine sandy bottom.
Three barracuda
circled a shoal,
Seychelle cowboys
moving their herd.

II.

Changi, Singapore 1971

They lay stretched out
on Changi Beach,
smoking.
He stroked
her fine sandy bottom
while crickets sang.
When the moon rose
they walked naked
across the grass,
looking out for snakes,
still lying to each other.

A LOVE SONG FOR MISS MUDIE

She walked through the door each morning
brightening that cold room with her warmth,
in her white shirt and tartan skirt
fastened with a safety pin.
Hunting Gordon, he later learned.
He was hunting Miss Mudie,
seeking her smile, welcoming her touch
gentle on his arm, the electric thrill
when his fingers brushed hers,
waiting for the slow smile
that started behind her eyes
and was meant just for him.
He knew nothing of her other life,
nor cared. It was enough
for his five year-old heart
to meet her eyes each day.

LETTER ENDINGS

What shallow insincerity
is wrapped in sincerely yours,
or lies within yours truly?
How much love are you sending?

Tell me who it is
you regard so kindly
while you write,
while I wait
like Penelope,
yours, faithfully.

POETS IN EXILE

They are dislocated from
the landscape of their birth
by war, famine, faith,
by acts of men and gods,
take refuge in their work
without the language of their birth.

Knowing what was left,
leave nothing
when they move again.

IN OUR SECOND-HAND BOOK SHOP

"I'm looking for love"
she breathed in my ear,
soft husky voice caressing.
So we sailed in the SPRAY
heading south, shedding clothes,
eyes locked. Then she said,
"Poetry or letters" – took the wind from my sails,
missed a beat, missed my boat
but will see it again. Will I see her again?

Such is the madness that walked through the door
searching for love in the order of books
or the chaos of grief, bending like starlight
nearing the sun as totally eclipsed
as my moment of hope.
It was a moment for all time,
though time is not the same for us all.
Each beat is a new beginning,
the end of all that went before.
That is a truth.
Is that the love you seek?
Did you find it, poised on the edge,
when our eyes locked,
when we stood together,
naked, in a room full of books?

BUYING PHILIP CORBET'S BOOKS

Boxes closed,
shelves empty.
A life's work
dismantled –
scattered
like ashes
to nurture
fresh minds.

EDEN

Delicious, he said,
taking a bite.
Eve kissed juice
from his lips.
Let's climb the tree, she said,
and eat ripe figs
in the warm sun.
I'll go first.

Delicious, he said,
taking another bite.
Eve kissed his lips.
Let's climb higher,
eat more figs,
drink some wine
and fuck in the warm sun.
I'll go first.

COLOUR FADES

We are narcissi picked in bud,
given water, put in light
where, slowly, we open,
fill a room with scent,
wither and die.

Or a single frangipani
plucked in bloom
and placed behind an ear –
crushed against a pillow,
found in the morning,
and placed with care
between leaves of a book
where colour fades.
Faint scent remains.

LAST POST

Outward-bound, off Senegal, the music died.
I closed my trumpet case on her letters,
packed alongside the shining brass.

At the guard-rail by the sea-boat
I held her hopes with both hands,
then dropped them overboard.

I watched the case float clear astern,
wondering if that last post would blow ashore.

ERRING AND STRAYING

Singing in the choir stall
she would blow him a kiss
with each perfectly enunciated
vowel or consonant.
Teasing with a glimpse of her tongue
between the softest of lips,
she would glance at him beneath
demurely lowered lids.
Or wrinkle a little her tilt-tipped nose,
or, as he waited to confess
his manifold sins and wickedness,
draw a deep breath that lifted
her tilt-tipped breasts
beneath her surplice,
beneath her blouse where, he knew,
she would be wearing white lace.
Naughty Mrs Taylor, the vicar's wife.

LIGHTING THE FIRST FIRE OF AUTUMN

Splitting sun-dried pine boards
sawn to length months ago,
resin-sweet scent fills the air.
Kindling springs from the axe,
falling like leaves at my feet.

Old headlines catch fire,
scattering words as ash.

Resin bubbles, pine spits, blackens,
bursts into scented light,
wakes memories of
hot days, olive groves,
nights sleeping under stars,
a bursting fig, hands cool in mine,
the kindness of the very poor.

JOINING THE NAVY – SEPTEMBER 1963

Crossing that river
we gave up our freedom.

Trained in our duties
we served at sea.
Some died.

Civilians were 'Outside'.
We pitied you.

HMS WAKEFUL VISITS HULL – DECEMBER 1964

Steaming up the muddy river
to berth among trawlers thick alongside,
the rich stink of cod hanging over the town,
hanging over the bustle of unloading
and clanging of hammers,
over the riveting, the whistles blowing,
over steam and smoke from factories,
over plants, cranes, trains,
over ships sailing on the tide
for fish-rich waters far away.

A boy in his uniform, freshly pressed,
shoes spat and polished, shirt starched,
white cap gleaming under sodium lights,
marched along the quay to the City Hall,
past bars full of smoke, old men yarning,
the young just home, filling up with beer,
looking for a fight, food, a fuck
before they sail on the next tide, drunk or sober.
The boy kept marching, up the steps of the City Hall.

The Lord Mayor's reception promised
food and beer and dancing to a band
in the towering cavern of the City Hall.
He only remembers meeting Peggy Fisher
in her tight black dress, with her permed black hair
and her soft white hands,
who took him to the dance floor
and held him ever closer to her soft white breasts.
The boy kept dancing on the polished floor of the City Hall.

Leaving the stink of fish and the muddy river,
old men yarning and Peggy Fisher,
a virgin sailor stood wrapped in his oilskins
on an open bridge in the cold North Sea.
He couldn't stop thinking of soft white breasts,
the tight black dress, of lips that promised –
wondering why he had kept on dancing
on the polished floor of the City Hall.

SIR GALAHAD

In this storm
lean on me.
I will hold you.
Put your hand in mine
and walk against the wind.
Do not flinch
or fear the blasts.

When it's calm
press your lips to mine.
Then we'll face the fire.

TRAFALGAR DAY

A buzzard hangs above the cliff,
feathers ragged in the wind;
sheers off, hangs again, anchored by
slight movements of its tail and wings.

Soaring up the zawn
choughs call, sharp and clear,
sweep low above the gorse,
tumble home out of sight.

There was no light on Wolf Rock
when Nelson sailed that last time,
nor when Pickle brought home
news of his death and victory.

A buzzard, hanging above the cliff,
ignored the sail far out to sea.
Choughs danced on the wind
and church bells rang.

SHOULDER TO SHOULDER

Marching shoulder to shoulder
they wheel and turn,
the sharp beat of nailed boots
echoes across the square.
Chins in, chests out, they march as one
towards the muttering guns.

Leaning shoulder to shoulder
against the trench wall
in the damp Picardy dawn,
eyes closed, heads bowed,
smoking as they wait to attack
the stuttering guns.

Now they lie where they fell,
in Regimental lines,
with perfect dressing by the right,
or in an unmarked grave,
or shoulder to shoulder with a Boche
beneath the Picardy sun.

11TH SEPTEMBER 2011

September the eleventh, ten years on,
the tail of Hurricane Katia
piles the ocean against our shores,
strips leaves from trees
to fly like papers from those towers.
Apples fall softly to the ground,
unlike jumpers from those towers.

Trees withstand the bullying wind,
storms blow out, seas calm.
If only man would do the same.

WRITING POETRY

I am having
open-heart surgery
without anaesthetic,
the naked beating of my heart
laid bare for all who care to see.
Or is it trepanning
without sanctity,
this journey
through my mind,
where strangers make
swift judgements
without thought.

"MISSING. CAN YOU HELP? "

Stephen Hadley, aged twenty-six,
missing from Walsall for eighteen months,
stares blankly along the Cornish coast.

So long without a word.

He was born in Devon.
Tall, slim, with cropped brown hair
and thin moustache.

Why is this poster here, on this cliff path?
How long before the wind plucks it down?

The flooding tide washes empty sand below.

It starts to rain.
Now there are tears in his lost blue eyes
which I wipe away as I turn to go.

THE WATER WAS WARM

She stood up in the sea
as he stopped at the edge,
a layer of sweat between them.
The tide rose.
Waves broke at their feet.
The water was warm.
Inhibitions held,
tight as limpets to a rock.
He moved to one side,
walked into the sea
as she came ashore.
Neither looked back.
Both sighed.

A PAINTING FOR MY UNBORN GRANDCHILD

Here is where your father walked and swam.
I hope one day you will swim here too,
walk these cliffs,
smell that warm earth, gorse
and honeyed scent of summer,
race your brother and sister across these sands,
build 'tain't gones', fall off waves,
have fish and chips for twenty seven,
all cousins, sleep in the quillet,
play screaming Pit on the Bowgie lawn,
then scramble down the Stickly Prickly Path,
hop boulders, jump into that icy pool,
and climb through the Count House window for tea.

YORKSHIRE RELISH

Men put ships in bottles, and spirits
sealed tight with wax and lead,
but not in this one
dug from the garden of a manse.

Its pale green neck proudly states
'Yorkshire Relish',
projecting an image of gritty fortitude,
tight-lipped and pursed,
of preachers living their joyless gritty lives
among the lawless miners of our Cornish town.

Now it holds an allium, a globe of violet stars,
whose stem was snapped, a ship dismasted,
cut loose, adrift in Yorkshire Relish,
dying where it stands.

WIRE TAPPING

A woodpecker clings
to a telegraph pole,
the last in Cot Valley,
tapping its urgent message
along wires which only carry
broadband or digital.

There are no longer telegraphists
listening to the hash of static,
fingers poised to answer
a burst of morse.
Wires hum, busy with spam.
This last woodpecker is not logged on –
its lonely call unanswered.

MIDSUMMER'S DAY

This is the last full day before
the sun begins its slow slide to winter.
From tomorrow
it will set a little further south
each day until December.
And yet, so much of summer
is still to come: holidays,
the harvest, fruit to pick,
blackberry flowers not yet set,
the warming sea, earth baked dry.

Children race across the sand
chasing dreams from year to year.

LOOKING ACROSS COT VALLEY IN JULY

Wind: *Calm*
Visibility: *300 feet*
Barometer: *1013 steady*

A slow moving warm front
settles a clammy, wet-wool mist
that blankets Cot Valley in a thick 'St Juster.'
It clings persistently to cliffs,
fills zawns, adits, shafts,
drowns sounds of the rushing stream,
muffles the Longships warning whistle.
Drizzle, caught in spiders' webs,
glints in diffused grey light.

Aircraft and birds are grounded.

Wet fingers of cloud creep through the house,
mildewing leather,
dampening clothes, paper, bedding,
settling red rust on ironwork and
verdigris on the dulled brass fender.

Another summer day.
The restless sea washes across empty beaches.

ABOVE PROGO

Wind:	*N 3*
Sea:	*Slight*
Visibility:	*Good*
Cloud:	*7/8 stratus breaking*
Barometer:	*995 rising slowly*

After the rain clouds lift and lighten.
Far to the west sun spills and beckons.

After rain the sky brightens,
grey strands whiten.
Crystals sparkle in the pewter sea.

After the rain spirits lighten.
Children skip from pool to pool,
laughter floating after the rain.

GRASSHOPPER

A very small brown grasshopper
rested on my right knee.
He stared at me a while
before slowly turning his back
to contemplate the sea.
He wasn't much bothered
when I poked him gently from behind,
moving forward a couple of paces
to resume his study.
When he left, he sprang away,
leaping yards into the grass.

If only men could be as calm,
and jump as far with such ease.

SUMMER 2011 – RIOTS IN ST JUST-IN-WEST PENWITH

Groups of twelve or more gulls
assembled in the square
to raid the bins.
Riotous and tumultuous they were,
ignoring proclamations, commands and shouted orders
to be silent, to disperse themselves
and peaceably to depart to their habitations,
or to their lawful business,
for they saw it to be their lawful business
to raid said bins for food thrown in,
being hungry and their habitations
not supplied with half-eaten pasties,
crisps or hevva cake.

Furthermore, those twelve or more gulls,
unlawfully, riotously and tumultuously
assembled together, to the disturbance
of the public peace, did oppose, obstruct,
let, hinder and hurt those persons
shouting at them, for which crime,
being adjudged felony
without the benefit of clergy,
and the offenders, those greedy gulls,
therein being adjudged felons,
are to suffer death as in the case of felony
without the benefit of clergy.
Not knowing this,
and anyway, always dying without the benefit of clergy,
those groups of twelve or more gulls
continued to raid bins,
sat on roofs and hurled abuse,
then took flight to shit on persons below.

DUSK IN NOVEMBER

Dusk in November
at Latitude 50° 07´ North 5° 40´ West.
Blowing ahead of the Front
on a cold South East wind,
strato-cu bubbles across the sky,
grey above the grey-green sea.
Kelp, piled high by recent storms, fills the cove.
A flash of orange, a broken fish box
lies among the wet brown strands.
A flash of red, the Longships lighthouse
gleams across white flecks of broken waves.
A pair of choughs, black clowns,
tumble home to roost.

Dusk in November
at Latitude 27° 28´ South 153° 02´ East
falls quickly,
no sun glowing pink
on the Western horizon.
No horizon.
Endless land, plains, mountains, desert,
swallows the sky.

An abrupt chorus of frogs,
singing above cicadas, greets the night.
A warm breeze lifts the scent of jasmine
under cotton-bud cunimb
drifting ashore from the wide Pacific.

Ten thousand, five hundred and five point seven miles
separate these two sunsets.
Today we talked by telephone.

MIDWINTER

The wind is north of west
on this rare calm day,
not stripping the willow
nor slates from my roof.
The sea is slight,
not dashing white horses
high up these cliffs.

Clouds crowd on the Scillies,
hiding the sun as it sets to its partner,
curtsies, is gone.
Earth spins on its axis,
turns to the moon.
The wind is north of west.
The light has gone.

DEATH OF A KINGFISHER

A kingfisher filled the sky
with iridescent blue
on its busy flight.

The bird died
above some muddy pool,
filling it with light,
turquoise and iridescent blue.

FUNERAL AT L'AQUILA – APRIL 2009

In the silent square
a small white coffin
sits on its parents' coffins,
another, slightly larger, lies beside,
waiting for the last piggy-back,
the last walk side-by-side,
the last rites
for childhood stilled
and parents killed
by trembling earth.

SMOKED MACKEREL

In your last unconscious moments
your faint breath was tainted
by the smoked fish smell
of corrupted flesh.

I had forgotten that smell
until I bought the fish,
forgotten the sound
of your laboured breathing,
the rattle as your lungs began to fill.

When it stopped,
silence filled the room.

DON'T WORRY

It squeezed my heart
when she said it,
that one small word.
Don't worry, Dad.
But how can you stop?
It's really OK, she said,
the biopsy's fine.
No worries.

12 June 2010, just after
Ellie rang from Brisbane

FAREWELL CHICA

No longer lumpy and limping
but racing the wind
through clouds of heaven
as she once stretched
to chase fresh scent
across tide-washed sand.

Not lying in your way
but leaping the surf,
or swimming deep pools
with stately grace
and otter-like steering,
or thump-thumping her greeting
with a hideous grin
to welcome you home.

Chica - good friend
July 1992 - 23 February 2006

HOLD ME

Each day blurs into another
much the same as the last
and the past few weeks.....
or is it years
since my son died?

Hold me a little longer
as you held me then
and tell me, my daughter,
what I am doing today
now that it's yesterday.

DEAD WASP

He was bowing to the glass,
wings curved behind
in supplication,
his head touching the sill,
crouching, as if in prayer,
a last desperate prayer
for the world outside.

LAMENT FOR THE DEATH OF A BULL
ALMERIA 1964

I saw a bull die
in the glare of the sun.
Stabbed through the lung
he bled to death in the sun,
leaning against the side of the ring
so he could not fall.

Blood poured from his mouth,
bright red in the sun,
brilliant against the sand in the ring,
sprayed on the walls when he raised his head,
shook his head, his great horns,
but less and less
as his blood flowed in the sun.

The crowd was silent,
watching the bull die slowly,
sink to his knees in the sun,
still leaning against the side of the ring
so he would not fall in the sun,
did not fall in the sun,
but lowered his head to his blood in the sand
with the sword in his lung,
and died in the sun.

LAMENT FOR THE DEATH OF A BADGER CUB
BOSORNE 2011

She was lying in the path, in a puddle, in the rain,
facing west, toward the sea, facing the rain,
her body hunched, awkward, black in the rain.
She lay still when my dog barked in her face,
lay still in the rain.

She cried when I tried to lift her muzzle,
to lift her head clear of the water
that puddled against her as she lay in the path,
unable to move,
drowning in the rain.

Standing behind her so she couldn't see,
I raised my right foot,
crushed her head with my heel,
knew death was quick, prayed for her soul,
wept in the rain.

RED ADMIRAL

He wasn't alone, lying there,
lips lifted in a faint smile.
There was also a butterfly
on the floor of that sterile room,
wings stretched out to catch the sun.
She placed it on the pillow
beside my father's head:
two sailors, one an Admiral.
Both dead.

IN THE ROOM WHERE MY MOTHER DIED

In the room where my mother died
a spider composes herself for death,
aligns her legs to the points of the compass
as she lies on her chestnut-brown back
on the wide slate sill in the winter sun.
When it is time, she folds her feet to her thorax
and departs her small, elegant life.

ALL THE ENERGY THE WORLD NEEDS

All the energy the world needs
is held within five oceans,
pent up for thousands of miles
before breaking on shore,
or hidden within the daily ebb and flow
of tides, regular as clockwork,
unstoppable.

Unlike the wind,
which stops blowing for days on end.
Imagine the world becalmed.

In the hottest of continents,
furthest from the sea,
heat and light pour down untapped.

It is a matter of organisation,
engineering and enterprise
to harness these gifts –
a matter of urgency too.

WATCHING WAVES BREAK OVER ROCKS

Fat women with round babies
lie in breaking waves
far below, their bodies
gleaming, naked and still,
some on their sides, others crouching,
heads pillowed on large thighs
or chubby arms.

Far offshore
a trawler heads north
to scour and plunder
scarce stocks of fish.

The sea washes over
fat women and babies
who lie there each tide.
They will be all that is fat
when the fish have gone.

BRITTANY – SEPTEMBER 2009

Here's how it is now:
a horse, galloping on a beach, dies,
poisoned by hydrogen sulphide
released by toxic algae.
A dog also dies.

A truck, filled with toxic weed
scooped from that beach,
crashes in the middle of a town,
spilling its foul cargo across the square.
The driver had collapsed.

Is it too late to save the dying sea?

THE LAND'S END

Would you look at the empty sea,
not a ship in sight
and this in the mouth of the Channel.
There is the Wolf, the Longships Light,
the horizon clear all round.
Where are the ships,
the cargoes, where is the trade?

Would you look at the restless sea
beating against this cliff,
the foam a coffee-brown,
tide-lines of plastic and scum.

Would you look at the fished-out sea
and think of the shoals you saw
boiling beneath your bows.
Would you think that men still fish,
clean oil tanks off-shore,
throw plastics overboard,
pump sewage from the land.

Should you look at this empty sea
it will be dying before your eyes.

THE END

Nothing was agreed.
Looking down from above
angels wept. Lands flooded.
Hurricanes blew when they sighed.

*written at the time of the Copenhagen conference
on climate change, December 2009.*

AND I AM HOME

It is May. The stream is full,
the wind cool, flowers bloom.
Gorse and alexander narrow the lane,
forget-me-nots reflect the sky
where swallows hunt,
and I am home.

Three weeks gone.
Unfurled bluebells hang
above thrift and squill.
Choughs call across the cove
where waves break soft
on mounds of rotting kelp.

My dog wakes an adder
basking in the sun,
then plays a deadly game,
provoking swift half strikes
at her teasing nose.
She jerks it back, just in time.

I thrust my jacket like a cape
between dog and snake.
Yellowy green and jagged black,
the adder rounds on me.

We stare at each other, stare and stare.
She curls away, slides swiftly out of sight
with a contemptuous flick of her tail,
and I walk home.

NOTES

SIR GALAHAD

Sir Galahad	-	Knight renowned for gallantry & purity
Sir Galahad	-	Landing Ship Logistics, bombed and set on fire in Bluff Cove, Falkland Islands, 8th June 1982 48 soldiers & ship's company killed.

Second Engineer Officer Paul Anderson Henry G.M. RFA

Three aircraft attacked Sir Galahad, causing devastating loss of life. One bomb went through an open hatch and exploded, creating a massive fireball that swept through the tank deck where the Welsh Guards were waiting to disembark. The second bomb exploded in the galley area, killing the butcher, Sung Yuk Fai, instantly and injuring several other crewmen. The third bomb burst in the engine room, killing Third Engineer Officer Andrew Morris. This last bomb produced thick clouds of choking smoke, trapping Third Engineer Officer Christopher Hailwood and Junior Engineer Officer Neil Bagnall in the Machinery Control Room. Junior Engineer Officer Bagnall attempted to escape from the engine room but was driven back by the smoke. Second Engineer Officer Paul Henry gave the only set of breathing apparatus to Junior Engineer Bagnall and ordered him to try again. He saved Neil Bagnall's life. Christopher Hailwood and Paul Henry died.
On the 11th October 1982, Second Engineer Officer Henry's family were presented with a Posthumous George Medal in recognition of his bravery.

I found this out after I had written the poem, when researching the title.

FUNERAL AT L'AQUILA
309 people died in the earthquake at L'Aquila

CORNISH WORDS USED IN THIS COLLECTION

Quillet: small paddock surrounded by a granite hedge

Adit: horizontal shaft, often driven in from the cliff or side of a valley for access to or to drain water from a mine.

Zawn: valley

LOCATION NOTES

Carn Gloose is the headland between Cot Valley and Cape Cornwall. I walk there every day.

Progo is the first cove south of Cot Valley.

Cot Valley runs down to the sea. Ancient mine workings define the landscape.